Wildflowers
of Colorado & Southern Wyoming

George Miller

Adventure Quick Guides

YOUR WAY TO EASILY IDENTIFY WILDFLOWERS

Adventure Quick Guides

This Adventure Quick Guide features 152 of the most common wildflowers you'll see in the southern Rockies, from the Laramie Mountains in southern Wyoming to the San Juan Mountains in southern Colorado.

With more than 1,000 species of wildflowers, this botanically rich area encompasses 5 major ecozones ranging from shortgrass prairies at 4,000 feet to foothill shrublands, montane forests, and alpine tundra above 11,500 feet. The guide's major emphasis is the showy flowers from the foothills through the spruce-fir forests and alpine meadows, the areas most popular for outdoor recreation with the most residential settings.

WILDFLOWERS OF COLORADO FIELD GUIDE

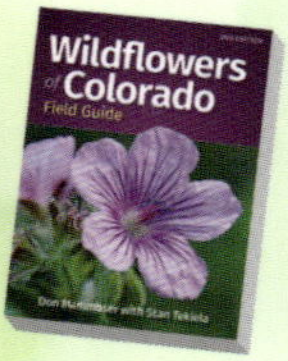

For more information about wildflowers, such as the season of bloom, habitat, fruit, and interesting gee-whiz facts, use Don Mammoser's field guide for Colorado. It features 200 species in all.

WILDFLOWERS OF THE ROCKY MOUNTAINS PLAYING CARDS

Improve your wildflower identification skills with these beautiful cards.

GEORGE MILLER

Longtime botanist and nature photographer George Miller has explored the West for 30 years and has been published in books, magazines, and newspapers. He's written 6 guidebooks to plants and animals of the Southwest, including the best-sellers *Landscaping with Native Plants of the Southwest* and *A Field Guide to Wildflowers, Trees, and Shrubs of Texas,* as well as 5 smartphone wildflower guides. He is president of the Albuquerque Chapter of the Native Plant Society of New Mexico, which includes southern Colorado.

10 9 8 7 6 5 4 3 2

Wildflowers of Colorado and Wyoming
Cover and book design by Lora Westberg
Edited by Brett Ortler
Cover image: Sticky Jacob's Ladder by George Miller

Printed in China
ISBN 978-1-59193-682-4 (book); 978-1-59193-683-1 (ebook)

KEY

- Wildflowers are sorted into 4 groups by color and organized within groups from smaller to larger blooms.
- Leaf attachment icons are shown next to each wildflower.
- Descriptions include important facts, such as cluster shape, number of petals or center color to help you quickly identify the species. Size information is sometimes included as well.

LEAF ATTACHMENT

Wildflower leaves attach to stems in different ways. The leaf icons next to the flowers show alternate, opposite, whorled, perfoliate, clasping, and basal attachments. Some wildflower plants have two or more types of leaf attachments.

ALTERNATE leaves attach in an alternating pattern.

OPPOSITE leaves attach directly opposite each other.

BASAL leaves originate at the base of the plant and are usually grouped in pairs or in a rosette.

PERFOLIATE leaves are stalkless and have a leaf base that completely surrounds the main stem.

CLASPING leaves have no stalk, and the base partly surrounds the main stem.

WHORLED leaves have three or more leaves that attach around the stem at the same point.

PARTS OF A FLOWER

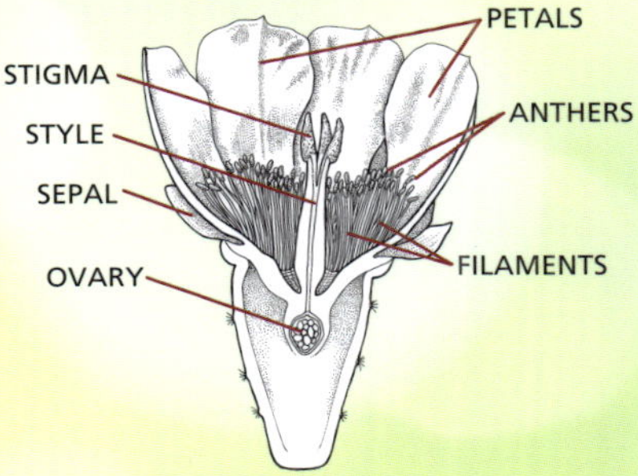

STIGMA
+ STYLE
PISTIL

ANTHERS
+ FILAMENTS
STAMENS

ELEVATION CHANGE AND PLANT DIVERSITY

Colorado and southern Wyoming are home to a vast matrix of plant communities. From north to south, the area spans 400 miles, and thanks to the towering Rocky Mountains, there are also profound differences in elevation, which dramatically affect plant populations. In fact, for every 1,000-foot increase in elevation, the average annual temperature drops 3 degrees and precipitation increases 1.5 inches–the equivalent of moving 600 miles northward. So if you want to spot a specific wildflower, keeping the elevation in mind is key.

With increasing elevation, the lower-lying grassland plains (now mostly farmland) give way to foothill shrublands, which occur from about 5,400 to 7,000 feet. Juniper, Sagebrush, Piñyon Pine, and Mountain Mahogany dominate the slopes and inter-mountain valleys, along with a host of wildflowers. Here, showy flowers include Rocky Mountain Beeplant, Western Wallflower, milkvetch, Dakota Vervain, and sunflowers.

At about 7,000 feet, shrublands transition into montane forests of Ponderosa Pine and Douglas Fir, which extend to 9,500 feet. Wildflowers thrive in the open understory and blanket meadows and streamsides. Look for monkshood, Jacob's Ladder, Rocky Mountain Penstemon, Sulphur Flower Buckwheat, Woods Rose, Scarlet Penstemon, Sky Rocket, and Shooting Stars.

From 9,500 to 11,500 feet, dense subalpine forests of spruce and fir cover the mountainsides. Luxuriant displays of wildflowers blanket meadows and open areas. Here you'll find Blue Columbine, Marsh Marigold, Barbey Larkspur, buttercups, both blue and white violets, lupines, Golden Pea, Fireweed, Fairy Slipper and Coralroot Orchids, and the head-high Monument Plant and Corn Lily.

At timberline, alpine flowers form clumps, carpets, mounds, and mats of glorious blooms from late June through July, often following the melting snow line. Across the treeless tundra, look for Elephant Head, Flowery Phlox, King's Crown, Avalanche Lily, Silky Phacelia, and Old-man-in-the-mountain.

Yellow to Orange

Berberis repens

Creeping Barberry

Groundcover; prickly, hollylike leaves; clusters of small, yellow flowers result in blue-black fruit

Cymopterus lemmonii

Mountain Parsley

Flower stems reach 2 feet tall; flat clusters of tiny flowers; parsleylike basal leaves

Eriogonum alatum

Winged Buckwheat

Tiny yellow flowers on mostly leafless stems that are 4 feet tall; winged seeds in tight clusters

Eriogonum umbellatum

Sulfur Flower Buckwheat

Clusters of yellow flowers on 12-inch leafless stems; dense mat of small, oval basal leaves

Gutierrezia sarothrae

Snakeweed/Broomweed

1–2-foot, rounded subshrub produces a bed of flowers; 3–8 tiny rays around a yellow disk

Lithospermum multiflorum

Many-flowered Puccoon

Curving clusters of showy tubular flowers crown clumps of erect stems; leaves narrow, pointed

Orthocarpus luteus

Yellow Owl-clover

Leafy spikes of club-shaped flowers on yellow-purple stems; 3 deep lobes on upper leaves

Senecio bigelovii

Nodding Ragwort

Nodding, budlike, yellow-maroon flower heads with no rays; tall stems with pointed leaves

Yellow to Orange

Solidago velutina

Three-nerve Goldenrod

Arching clusters of tiny yellow flowers on tall stems; upper leaves with 3 strong nerves

Agoseris aurantiaca

Orange False-dandelion

Dandelion-size orange flowers grow on leafless stalks from a basal rosette; milky sap

Amauriopsis dissecta

Ragleaf Bahia

Flowers have stubby, petallike rays around a yellow disk; branching stems; narrow, lobed leaves

Dasiphora fruticosa

Shrubby Cinquefoil

Shrub covered with showy flowers with 5 yellow petals; leaves with small, radiating, pointed leaflets

Draba aurea

Golden Draba

Short stems with round clusters of small flowers; hairy leaves; fruit is a small, slightly twisted pod

Erysimum capitatum

Wallflower

Round clusters of yellow or red-orange flowers on tall stems; long, erect seedpods hug stems

Geum rossii

Alpine Avens

Flowers have 5 rounded petals, many stamens, and fernlike basal leaves; common in subalpine to alpine habitats

Grindelia squarrosa

Curlycup Gumweed

1–3-foot bushy stems; resinous flower heads with or without yellow rays; oblong leaves with blunt teeth

Hymenoxys richardsonii

Pingue Rubberweed

Short yellow rays with 3 lobes; yellow disk; leaves up to 6 inches long with filament-like segments

Mimulus guttatus

Yellow Monkey Flower

Tubular, bright yellow flowers with a heavily bearded middle lobe with red spots; favors wet areas

Oreochrysum parryi

Parry's Goldenweed

Leafy flower heads have slender rays around disk florets; stems hairy; leaves broad and pointed

Packera fendleri

Notchleaf Ragwort

Clusters of yellow flower heads with slender rays on a lone; hairy stem; leaves woolly, cut to midrib

Pedicularis bracteosa

Fern-leaf Lousewort

Showy spikes of yellow to reddish tubular flowers with a tiny hood; tall stems; fernlike leaves

Polemonium brandegeei

Yellow Sky Pilot

Yellow to white, funnel-shaped flowers on 10-inch stems; leaves have small oval leaflets on midrib

Potentilla anserina

Silverweed Cinquefoil

Prostrate plants with 5-petal flowers send out red runners; leaves with narrow, toothed leaflets along midrib

Potentilla hippiana

Woolly Cinquefoil

Erect stems bear flowers with 5 yellow petals; toothed leaflets spaced along midrib; bottoms are silvery-hairy

Ranunculus inamoenus

Fanleaf Buttercup

Small, rounded petals surround a greenish cone with many yellow anthers; leaves rounded

Potentilla pulcherrima.

Slender Cinquefoil

Erect stems; flowers with 5 yellow petals; leaflets radiate from a central point and silvery beneath

Ranunculus macauleyi

Rocky Mountain Buttercup

Yellow flowers over a cup of dense, black, hairy sepals; elliptical leaves with teeth at tip

Sedum lanceolatum

Lanceleaf Stonecrop

Small, yellow flowers with red highlights; short stems; leaves are succulent, green-red, cylindrical

Senecio atratus

Black-tipped Ragwort

Clusters of yellow flowers and black-tipped buds on hairy stems; leaves gray-green, broad, pointed

Senecio eremophilus

Cutleaf Ragwort

Yellow flowers have black-tipped buds; stems are tall, often reddish and branching; leaves deeply cut

Senecio triangularis

Arrowleaf Ragwort

Tall, bushy stems; clusters of flowers with 8 slender rays around a yellow disk; toothed leaves are triangular with a flat base

Tetraneuris acaulis

Alpine Stemless Daisy

Solid yellow flowers on leafless stalks have 3-toothed rays; leaves a crowded basal mat; surfaces often silvery and hairy

Yellow to Orange

Thermopsis montana

Golden Pea

Spikes of golden, pealike flowers crown 1–2-foot tall stems; leaves with 3 leaflets

Verbascum thapsus

Mullein

Crowded spikes of small, yellow flowers on tall stems; large, fuzzy basal leaves; exotic; along roads

Hypericum scouleri

St. John's Wort

Rounded clusters of flowers; yellow petals and many stamens; 2-foot stems; found in moist soils

Arnica cordifolia

Heart-leaf Arnica

Meadow flower with single 2-foot hairy stem; one yellow flower; 2–4 pairs of heart-shaped leaves

Arnica mollis

Rough-leaf Arnica

12 inches tall; 2–4 pairs of rough, hairy, lance-shaped leaves; showy flower heads; colonizes meadows

Erythronium grandiflorum

Avalanche Lily

Nodding yellow flowers with petals curled backwards; leafless stems; two oval basal leaves

Heliomeris multiflora

Showy Goldeneye

Tall, branching stems bear numerous 1–2-inch-wide, solid yellow flower heads; leaves narrow, pointed

Heterotheca villosa

Hairy Golden Aster

Arrays of solid yellow flower heads cover dense clumps of stems; leaves are short, hairy, widely spaced

Hymenoxys grandiflora

Old-man-in-the-mountain

Low-growing with 1–2 inches wide, yellow flowers with many 3-toothed rays; very woolly stems

Pyrrocoma crocea

Orange Skyflower

Showy orange to bright yellow flower heads; 2-inch-wide blooms; 2-foot stems; leathery leaves

Rudbeckia laciniata

Cutleaf Coneflower

Tall plant with narrow yellow rays around yellow, conical disk; leaves deeply cut along midrib

Helianthella quinquenervis

Five-nerve Dwarf Sunflower

Tall stems usually have a single, nodding, solid-yellow flower head; leaves pointed; 3–5 major veins

Helianthus annuus

Common Sunflower

Tall stems with many flowers; yellow rays around a brown disk; heart-shaped leaves can be large

Helianthus petiolaris

Prairie Sunflower

Robust stems; many flowers; yellow rays around a brown disk; lance-shaped leaves can be large

Hymenoxys hoopesii

Orange Sneezeweed

Yellow-orange flower heads have slender, drooping rays around a yellow disk; leaves are broad and clasping

Rudbeckia hirta

Black-eyed Susan

Ray flowers solid yellow or with red splotches surround a conical brown disk, or "eye"; leaves hairy, lance-shaped

Allium cernuum

Nodding Onion

Nodding clusters of urn-shaped, pink-white flowers; leafless stalks; grasslike leaves smell like onion

Allium geyeri

Geyer's Onion

Erect clusters of pink to white, urn-shaped flowers; leafless stalks; grasslike leaves smell like onion

Asclepias speciosa

Showy Milkweed

Clusters of rose-pink flowers; stems are 2–4 feet with milky sap; seedpods coated by warty prickles

Lewisia pygmaea

Pygmy Bitterroot

Pink petals; short stems; ground-hugging; found in high meadows; long, narrow leaves

Pedicularis procera

Giant Lousewort

Stems reach 7 feet tall; dense spikes of tubular, red-streaked flowers; leaves fernlike

Rhodiola integrifolia

King's Crown

Clusters of dark-red flowers crown tips of tall stems crowded with pointed, succulent leaves

Rumex densiflorus

Dense-flowered Dock

Slender, showy spikes of red, disklike seeds cover tall stems; a rosette of broad basal leaves

Silene acaulis

Moss Campion

Small flowers with 5 pink petals form dense mats or mounds above timberline; leaves are short and grasslike

Red to Pink

Astragalus missouriensis

Missouri Milkvetch

Clusters of pink flowers with white centers on 6-inch stalks; pods oblong; stems to 5 feet long

Geranium richardsonii

Wild Geranium

Small flowers; 5 pinkish-white petals; slender pods pointed like a crane's bill; leaves lobed

Geum triflorum

Prairie Smoke/ Old Man's Whiskers

Red stalks have 3 nodding, urnlike flowers; feathery seed clusters

Hedysarum occidentale

Western Chainpod/ Sweetvetch

Shrubby; spikes of tubular flowers; chains of round seedpods

Peritoma serrulata

Rocky Mountain Beeplant

Tall stems; clusters of pink-purple flowers; long, drooping pods; leaves with 3 radiating leaflets

Trifolium parryi

Parry Clover

Compact, spherical heads of pink and white flowers; tall stems; leaves have 3 leaflets

Calypso bulbosa

Fairy Slipper Orchid

A single, flamboyant pink, 1-inch flower; leafless, 5-inch stalk; one oval basal leaf

Castilleja miniata

Scarlet Paintbrush

Spikes of red, pitchfork-lobed bracts; flowers are small, yellow, and beak-shaped; stems reach 2 feet tall

Red to Pink

Castilleja rhexifolia

Rosy Paintbrush

Hairy spikes; small, green, beaklike flowers; pink-magenta bracts; strongly veined, broad leaves

Chamerion angustifolium

Fireweed

Spikes of pink flowers on leafy, chest-high stems; forms dense stands on open slopes

Ipomopsis aggregata

Skyrocket

Clusters of red, trumpetlike flowers; spreading petals with white spots on throat; leaves threadlike

Penstemon barbatus

Scarlet Bugler Penstemon

1–3-foot stems; spikes of tubular flowers; bottom petals bent back for hummingbird pollination

Sphaeralcea coccinea

Scarlet Globemallow

Low, bushy plant with small, pink, orange, or red flowers; notched petals; leaves cut into thin lobes

Aquilegia elegantula

Western Red Columbine

Nodding red flowers with petals tipped with yellow; long red spurs on stems reaching 2 feet tall

Erigeron elatior

Tall Fleabane

Numerous pink-tinged to lavender rays; a yellow disk on a 1–2-foot stem; buds nodding; flower cup white-woolly

Rosa woodsii

Woods Rose

Pink flowers have showy clusters of yellow stamens; stems thorny; leaves have 5–7 oval leaflets along midvein

Red to Pink

White to Green

Achillea millefolium

Common Yarrow

Flat to rounded clusters of tiny, white flowers crown 1–3-foot-tall stems; leaves aromatic, fernlike

Anaphalis margaritacea

Pearly Everlasting

Pearly white flowers, some with yellow florets in the center; stems densely hairy; leaves narrow

Antennaria parvifolia

Pussytoes

Tiny, woolly, white flowers that don't spread open; short stems from a mat of hairy basal leaves

Asclepias subverticillata

Poison Milkweed

Small, starlike flowers; stems up to 40 inches; linear, slender leaves in whorls of 3–4; milky sap

Bistorta bistortoides

American Bistort

Cylindrical spikes of small, white to pink flowers on tall stems; long, elliptic, pointed leaves

Cardamine cordifolia

Heart-leafed Bittercress

Rounded clusters of tiny flowers with 4 petals; tall stems; found in wet areas; leaves heart-shaped

Cerastium arvense

Field Chickweed

Clusters of tiny flowers with 5 white, 2-lobed petals; 12-inch stems; leaves slender to lance-shaped; forms clumps

Cicuta maculata

Water Hemlock

Clusters of tiny, white flowers on 2–9-foot smooth stems, often with purple streaks; DEADLY POISONOUS

White to Green

Conioselinum scopulorum

Hemlock Parsley

Round clusters of tiny white flowers in an umbrellalike array; stems can reach 3 feet tall in wet places

Corallorhiza maculata

Spotted Coralroot Orchid

Small, red-spotted, white flowers cover the upper half of red or yellow, pencil-thin stems

Goodyera oblongifolia

Rattlesnake Plantain Orchid

8-inch bloom stalk; tiny white flowers; basal rosette of oval leaves with a white midvein

Hydrophyllum fendleri

Fendler's Waterleaf

Dense round clusters of flowers on hairy, 3-foot stems; leaves with 9–13 lobed leaflets along midrib

Ligusticum porter

Oshá

Umbrella-shaped clusters of tiny white flowers; robust stems with large parsleylike leaves

Maianthemum stellatum

Star Solomon's Seal

Loose clusters with one star-shaped flower per tiny branch; stems have swordlike leaves

Micranthes rhomboidea

Diamond-leaf Saxifrage

Small cluster of white flowers with 5 petals; leafless stalk; basal leaves broadly oval to triangular

Phacelia heterophylla

Varileaf Phacelia

Bristly clusters of creamy flowers have extended, hairlike stamens; leaves are hairy, elliptical, and strongly veined

White to Green

Valeriana acutiloba

Sharpleaf Valerian

Rounded clusters of white-pink flowers; stems 8–30 inches tall; 1–2 widely spaced pairs of leaves

Anticlea elegans

Mountain False Death Camas

Creamy-greenish flowers; stems 1–2 feet; grasslike leaves; toxic

Erigeron coulteri

Coulter's Fleabane

Numerous slender, white rays around a yellow disk; stems hairy, 1–2 feet; leaves lance-shaped

Erigeron divergens

Spreading Fleabane

White to lavender-tinted rays around a yellow disk; branching stems; buds nod; narrow leaves

Erigeron melanocephalus

Black-head Fleabane

White rays around a yellow disk; dense, black hairs; one flower per stem; spatula-shaped leaves

Fragaria vesca

Wild Strawberry

Small, white flowers and red fruits; basal leaves with 3 leaflets with coarse teeth

Heracleum maximum

Cow Parsnip

Umbrella-shaped clusters of small, white flowers; stems to 8 feet tall; leaves with 3 broad, pointed lobes

Lathyrus lanszwertii

White Peavine

Pealike flowers with red veins on upper petals; sprawling to upright stems; leaves with 4–10 leaflets paired along midrib

White to Green

Noccaea fendleri

Wild Candytuft

Round clusters of small, white flowers with purplish buds; short stems; clasping, pointed leaves

Pedicularis racemosa

Sickle-top Lousewort

Long clusters of creamy to pink flowers with a downward-curving upper lobe; pointed leaves

Phlox multiflora

Flowery Phlox

Small, white to bluish flowers with 5 rounded petals; narrow, pointed leaves; mat-like plant

Veratrum californicum

Corn Lily

Small flowers on branching stalks; tall, cornlike stems in moist areas; broad, strongly veined leaves

Viola canadensis

Canada Violet

White flower with narrow, spreading petals and a yellow throat; short stems; heart-shaped leaves

Caltha leptosepala

Marsh Marigold

Purple buds, white petals, many yellow stamens; leaves heart-shaped, fleshy; in wet areas

Frasera speciosa

Monument Plant

Whorls of purple-spotted green flowers; 2–6-foot stalks rise from a dense basal rosette, which has broad leaves

Rubus parviflorus

Thimbleberry

White flowers and red, edible berries hide amid leafy, thornless shrub; the broad leaves have pointed lobes

White to Green

Sidalcea candida

White Checker Mallow

Clusters of 2-inch-wide, hibiscus-like flowers; tall stems; leaves with radiating lobes; found in wet areas

Townsendia exscapa

Stemless Easter Daisy

Clusters of stemless, daisylike flowers; yellow centers; grows in dense mats of narrow leaves

Trollius albiflorus

White Globe Flower

Creamy flowers with showy yellow anthers; long stems; leaves with pointed lobes; in wet meadows

Anemone canadensis

Canada Anemone

5 petals, many whitish anthers; leaves with 3 deep lobes; a whorl of leaves midway up stem

Calochortus gunnisonii

Gunnison's Mariposa Lily

Cup-shaped flowers with a purplish band and yellow hairs; leafless stems; leaves grasslike

Leucanthemum vulgare

Ox-eye Daisy

This exotic daisy escaped gardens and now displaces native plants in roadsides and meadows

Oenothera caespitosa

Tufted Evening Primrose

Slender, pointed buds and showy flowers; 4 heart-shaped petals grow on sprawling stems

Pulsatilla patens

Pasque Flower

Shaggy stems have white to light blue flowers above a whorl of narrow leaves and deeply lobed basal leaves

Blue to Purple

Cirsium undulatum

Wavyleaf Thistle

Lavender to creamy, tassellike flowers with short, yellow spines beneath; 1–3-foot woolly stems

Cirsium vulgare

Bull Thistle

Showy, spiny clusters of purple, tassellike flowers; stems branching, spiny, and up to 6 feet tall

Glandularia bipinnatifida

Dakota Vervain

Rounded clusters of small, tubular, pink-purple flowers with notched petals; leaves with pointed lobes

Lupinus argenteus

Silvery Lupine

Spikes of purple to blue, pealike flowers crown leafy stems; leaves with 6–9 radiating leaflets

Mertensia lanceolata

Lanceleaf Bluebells

Clusters of tubular flowers hang from arching stems 4–16 inches tall; pointed, slender leaves

Mirabilis albida

Velvet Umbrellawort

Clusters of 3 flowers with variable color; long stamens; branching stems with dark, glandular hairs

Pedicularis groenlandica

Elephant Head

Dense spikes with small, showy flowers resembling a tiny elephant's head; leaves fernlike; favors wet areas

Phacelia sericea

Silky Phacelia

Dense spikes of showy purple flowers have extended, hairlike stamens; leaves are silky-hairy and fernlike

Blue to Purple

Blue to Purple

Swertia perennis

Star Gentian

Star-shaped flowers; stem leaves clasping; basal leaves broad, smooth; favor wet areas

Synthyris alpina

Alpine Kittentails

Clusters of small, purplish flowers form woolly spikes on short stems; wrinkled, clasping leaves

Veronica wormskjoldii

Alpine Speedwell

Clusters of small flowers with 4 blue petals; elliptic, pointed leaves; grows in high meadows

Viola adunca

Hooked-spur Violet

Blue to violet flowers have white throats with dark lines; basal leaves oval to triangular

Astragalus crassicarpus

Groundplum Milkvetch

Clusters of purplish to pink flowers; sprawling stems reach 2 feet long; fruit is a plumlike pod

Dalea purpurea

Purple Prairie-Clover

Clusters of small, purple flowers bloom from bottom up; 8–36-inch stems; 3–7 leaflets along midrib

Dieteria canescens

Purple Aster

Flower heads have many slender, blue to purple rays around a yellow disk; leaves are linear to lance-shaped

Geranium caespitosum

Purple Geranium

Small, showy flowers have 5 petals, often curled back, and a protruding center; leaves are rounded, deeply lobed

Blue to Purple

Liatris punctata

Blazing Star

Spikes of thin, lavender flowers cover clumps of 1–3-foot stems; slender leaves around stem

Linum lewisii

Blue Flax

Delicate flowers last a day; pointed buds produce flowers; narrow, pointed leaves hug the stem

Monarda fistulosa

Beebalm

A whorl of blue to pink tubular flowers; 1–3-foot branching stems; lance-shaped leaves

Oxytropis lambertii

Purple Locoweed

Clusters of tubular, pealike flowers; leafless stalks; hairy leaves with paired leaflets along midrib

Penstemon strictus

Rocky Mountain Penstemon

Long spikes of blue-purple, tubular flowers grow on one side of a tall stem; pointed narrow leaves

Penstemon whippleanus

Dusky Penstemon

Whorled clusters of reddish purple, tubelike flowers with white stripes and hairs; clasping stem leaves

Primula parryi

Parry's Primrose

Clusters of dainty magenta flowers with yellow throats with a skunky aroma; leaves basal, broad, pointed

Primula pauciflora

Shooting Star

With swept-back magenta petals and a protruding filament tube, this flower of wet areas earns its common name

Blue to Purple

Prunella vulgaris

Self-heal

Short spikes of small, hooded flowers with a fringed lower lobe; elliptical leaves; forms colonies

Polemonium viscosum

Sticky Jacob's Ladder

Clusters of funnel-shaped, blue-violet flowers; whorled, fetid-smelling leaflets

Campanula rotundifolia

Harebell

Clusters of purple, bell-shaped flowers on slender, branching stems up to 2 feet tall; grasslike leaves

Clematis columbiana

Columbia Rock Clematis

Low-climbing vine with pale blue to purple nodding petals; seed bundle with long, silky tails

Clematis hirsutissima

Hairy Leatherflower

Hairy, urn-shaped flowers; hairy vining stems that reach 2 feet tall; seed head a cluster with silky tails

Erigeron formosissimus

Beautiful Fleabane

Numerous lavender to white rays surround a yellow disk; 4–16-inch stem; narrow leaves clasp stem

Erigeron speciosus

Pretty Fleabane

Numerous blue to lavender rays surround a yellow disk on 1–2-foot stems; leaves even-sized and oval to lance-shaped

Gentiana affinis

Pleated Gentian

Tubular flowers with blue-lines; never open widely; stems short; leaves narrow to oval

Blue to Purple

Gentiana parryi

Mountain Gentian

Clusters of tubular flowers with white throats and 5 blue petals; pointed, clasping leaves

Gentianopsis thermalis

Fringed Gentian

Flowers have 4 petals with fringed edges, twisted like pinwheels; lance-shaped leaves

Polemonium foliosissimum

Tall Jacob's Ladder

Rounded clusters of bell-shaped flowers on upper half of stems; leaves with pointed leaflets

Aconitum columbianum

Columbian Monkshood

Showy flowers with hoodlike upper petals; stems 1–6 feet; deeply cut leaves; all parts toxic

Aquilegia coerulea

Blue Columbine

Blue and white flowers with spreading petals and long spurs; stems 1–3 feet; 3-lobed leaves

Delphinium barbeyi

Barbey's Larkspur

Showy blue to purple flowers with tiny spurs; 2–5-foot stems; round leaves with 5–7 pointed lobes

Iris missouriensis

Missouri Iris

Classic iris flowers with blue-streaked petals bloom on stems from a basal cluster of long, slender leaves

Symphyotrichum foliaceum

Leafy-bracted (Alpine) Aster

Oval, leafy bracts cup flower heads with blue rays and yellow disks; broad, clasping leaves are widely spaced on 2-foot stems

Adventure Quick Guides

Only Colorado and Southern Wyoming Wildflowers

Organized by color
for quick and easy identification

Simple and convenient—narrow your choices by color and leaf attachment, and view just a few wildflowers at a time

- Pocket-size format—easier than laminated foldouts
- Professional photos of flowers in bloom
- Similar colors grouped together to ensure that you quickly find what you're looking for
- Leaf icons for comparison and identification
- Easy-to-use information for even casual observers
- Expert author who is a longtime botanist and a skilled nature photographer

NATURE / WILDFLOWERS / WEST

ISBN 978-1-59193-682-4 $9.95 U.S.
50995
9 781591 936824

Adventure Publications
an imprint of AdventureKEEN